American Trucks

of the 1960s

Those were the days ...™

VELOCE

Also from Veloce –

Those Were The Days ... Series
Alpine Trials & Rallies 1910-1973 (Pfundner)
American 'Independent' Automakers – AMC to Willys 1945 to 1960
(Mort)
American Station Wagons – The Golden Era 1950-1975 (Mort)
American Trucks of the 1950s (Mort)
American Trucks of the 1960s (Mort)
American Woodies 1928-1953 (Mort)
Anglo-American Cars from the 1930s to the 1970s (Mort)
Austerity Motoring (Bobbitt)
Austins, The last real (Peck)
Brighton National Speed Trials (Gardiner)
British and European Trucks of the 1970s (Peck)
British Drag Racing – The early years (Pettitt)
British Lorries of the 1950s (Bobbitt)
British Lorries of the 1960s (Bobbitt)
British Touring Car Racing (Collins)
British Police Cars (Walker)
British Woodies (Peck)
Café Racer Phenomenon, The (Walker)
Don Hayter's MGB Story – The birth of the MGB in MG's Abingdon
Design & Development Office (Hayter)
Drag Bike Racing in Britain – From the mid '60s to the mid '80s (Lee)
Dune Buggy Phenomenon, The (Hale)
Dune Buggy Phenomenon Volume 2, The (Hale)
Endurance Racing at Silverstone in the 1970s & 1980s (Parker)

Hot Rod & Stock Car Racing in Britain in the 1980s (Neil)
Last Real Austins 1946-1959, The (Peck)
Mercedes-Benz Trucks (Peck)
MG's Abingdon Factory (Moylan)
Motor Racing at Brands Hatch in the Seventies (Parker)
Motor Racing at Brands Hatch in the Eighties (Parker)
Motor Racing at Crystal Palace (Collins)
Motor Racing at Goodwood in the Sixties (Gardiner)
Motor Racing at Nassau in the 1950s & 1960s (O'Neil)
Motor Racing at Oulton Park in the 1960s (McFadyen)
Motor Racing at Oulton Park in the 1970s (McFadyen)
Motor Racing at Thruxton in the 1970s (Grant-Braham)
Motor Racing at Thruxton in the 1980s (Grant-Braham)
Superprix – The Story of Birmingham Motor Race (Page & Collins)
Three Wheelers (Bobbitt)

Great Cars
Austin-Healey – A celebration of the fabulous 'Big' Healey (Piggott)
Jaguar E-type (Thorley)
Jaguar Mark 1 & 2 (Thorley)
Triumph TR – TR2 to 6: The last of the traditional sports cars (Piggott)

Truckmakers
DAF Trucks since 1949 (Peck)
Mercedes-Benz Trucks (Peck)

www.veloce.co.uk

First published in April 2010 by Veloce Publishing Limited, Veloce House, Parkway Farm Business Park, Middle Farm Way, Poundbury, Dorchester, Dorset, DT1 3AR, England. Reprinted July 2017.
Fax 01305 250479/e-mail info@veloce.co.uk/web www.veloce.co.uk or www.velocebooks.com.

ISBN: 978-1-787111-72-1 UPC: 6-36847-01172-7

Contents

Preface

There are many good people to thank for helping to produce *American Trucks of the 1960s*. My son and collaborator, Andrew Mort, was once again essential in putting together this book. He personally handled all the images – scanning, enhancing, cropping, recording, filing, and packaging – as well as accompanied me on trips shooting and collecting information.

While Andrew was responsible for most of the colour shots of the restored trucks, it was truck enthusiasts and collectors, such as Norman Wood, C Dan Pannell, Mario Palma, George, Kevin and Charlie Tackaberry and Peter Vanderlinden, as well as GM Smith Ltd, Ford Motor Company, Chrysler Corporation, and Freightliner, who helped make this book come together. Special thanks go to Doug Grieve, whose personal photographic collection and knowledge of some of the rarest trucks was invaluable. Additional thanks also to Rod Grainger and his expert team at Veloce Publishing.

Even in trucking, film and television celebrities, such as Don Knotts, were often utilised to endorse various makes.
(Doug Grieve Collection)

Introduction

This "Those Were the Days ..." edition examines the American truck manufacturers and industry in the 1960s. It was a period of great innovation, growth, and prosperity, yet, as the decade progressed, increased market competition once again transformed the trucking industry. By the end of the 1960s many old names in the trucking business had disappeared, or became nothing more than a nameplate. Although 1969 was a banner year for the industry in regards to output, many truck manufacturers were facing serious financial problems. Increased manufacturing and development costs, stiff competition in niche and traditional markets, and additional safety and highway regulations were resulting in minimal profits or substantial losses for even the major truck manufacturers, despite higher production. The next decade would see additional consolidation and more once-proud names disappear.

US/Avoirdupois weight:
2000 pounds = 1 ton = 907kg

There was tremendous growth within the American trucking industry during the 1960s, as well as expansion, consolidation, standardization, regulation, and innovation. (Andrew Mort)

American trucks of the 1960s
More expansion, consolidation, standardisation, regulation, and innovation

By 1960, the trucking industry in North America had undergone a complete metamorphosis due to expansion, consolidation, standardisation, and regulations, and over the ensuing decade these factors continued to have a significant impact.

The number of major American truck manufacturers had shrunk to twenty-five by 1960, compared to thirty-two in 1950, and reduced further to seventeen by 1970. Still, trucking remained a growth industry. In 1960, truck production was 1,202,011 trucks, including buses, and by 1969 that number had increased to 1,918,519 units.

The US highway expansion program that came into effect in the 1950s continued to be supported and encouraged by the United States federal government, and further developed by state legislatures, although the new, 1960 Kennedy administration had its own slightly modified version of a transportation program.

In 1961, approximately 11,000 miles (17,700km) of interstate highways were constructed, and by

State and federal regulations often slowed the wheels of progress in the truck industry, but, throughout the decade, governments at both levels addressed these concerns. (Doug Grieve Collection)

1964 that figure had nearly doubled to over 20,000 miles (32,000km). By 1970, a total of 30,000 miles (48,000km) of interstate highway had been completed.

Despite taxing highway usage, it was not surprising that the entire program was running at a deficit of over three billion dollars by 1964. Still, President Johnson signed a bill that year authorising a further $840 million to build 2300 miles (3701km) of highway and 1000 miles (1609km) of access roads in eleven states in the eastern United States. Alas, by the end of the decade, the federal and state governments were forced to cut back due to dramatic increases in the annual inflation rate.

There were other government decisions directly affecting the trucking industry. While intense competition led to further mergers and consolidation,

it became obvious that in many cases state laws were hampering growth, as well as unnecessarily increasing the cost of shipping goods and materials by truck, which ultimately affected all Americans. President Kennedy was the first to strongly recommend the rescinding of rate regulations for the transporting of any bulk, agriculture and fishery freight. In 1964 the US Department of Commerce formally asked state governments to increase the weight and dimension limits for trucks using these highways.

State laws were slow to change, but by the end of the decade it was finally possible to ship goods via a set of doubles coast-to-coast using the thruway system.

Overall, the increase in government regulations had both a positive and negative benefit as far as truck manufacturers and operators were concerned. On the negative side there was plenty of bureaucracy. For example, in 1961 an interstate freight operator transporting goods coast-to-coast who operated in an 18-state area carried 136 items of identification in plates, papers, inspection forms, etc.

The decade was also filled with new safety regulations. For example, in 1960, laws were passed governing the use of separate turn signal systems front and rear, while at the same time acting as a hazard warning lights. Reflective markings were also required on the backs of trucks and trailers to reduce the risk of rear-end collisions.

The decade was also crammed with new safety regulations. For example, the Interstate Commerce Commission (ICC) introduced the uniform markings requirement on all vehicles carrying dangerous materials. Although both steel and aluminium tanks were built, by 1969, of the 2757 tanks built, 2260 were made of aluminium. (Doug Grieve Collection)

The 1960s saw the virtually universal use of fibreglass in truck cabs, as well as utilisation of plastics in truck and trailer construction. Featured here is a White 5000. (Doug Grieve Collection)

In addition, 1966 federal safety bills were enacted under the Johnson administration, as was the establishment of the Department of Transport. At the end of 1967 the DoT announced twelve motor vehicle safety proposals of which eight would take effect by December 1968. The remaining four came into law by December 1969. Although mostly directed toward the automobile industry, these new regulations also impacted on the trucking industry.

During the 1960s weight reduction continued to be

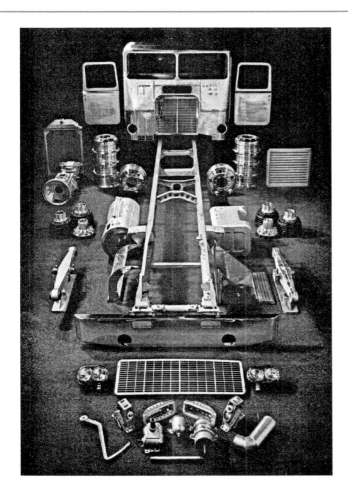

As well as plastics and fibreglass, lightweight aluminium was utilised in more and more truck parts, as shown in this advertisement from Freightliner. (Doug Grieve Collection)

a major element in design. New methods and materials were introduced, as well as an ever-increasing use of aluminium and fibreglass in trucks. The use of plastics in truck and trailer construction increased steadily due to its weight saving, lower initial, as well as maintenance costs, and longer service life. At the same time, some

old ideas were reintroduced, such as the softer-riding air suspension that fell out of favour in 1950s.

Innovative ideas in trucking continued to be introduced, and many were adopted industry-wide, whilst others failed to make an impact.

Multifuel engines were developed with General Motors leading the way in 1961. GM also offered kits to convert diesel engines to multifuel. Chrysler had been taking a different tact by further developing its gas turbine engine. A Dodge 'Turbo Power' truck underwent tests throughout the winter of 1961-62 with some impressive results, but by the late 1960s Chrysler's entire turbine car and truck program would be abandoned.

At the same time, many others – including General Motors – also felt that the turbine engine held promise in trucks and buses, and began developing experimental haulers. GM's was known as the Bison, and was unveiled at the 1964 New York Auto Show boasting a 1000hp turbine engine. This was followed by GM's Chevrolet Division unveiling its 'space age' Turbo Titan III truck of tomorrow at the New York World's Fair. Freightliner also built its first turbine engine in 1966, and Ford finally got into the gas turbine program with a prototype unveiled in 1969.

Yet, by the end of the decade, it was the gasoline V8 engine that was still the most popular choice, with 67 per cent of the truck market. Also steadily increasing in sales were the more efficient and longer-lasting diesel engines.

Many of the innovations of the 1960s were

Decking became the popular way to transport trucks from manufacturer to dealer. Here are three Dodges being moved by a transport company to another depot. (Doug Grieve Collection)

Piggybacking was also on the increase, and by 1962 over 25,000 trailers had been built. As the decade evolved, piggybacking combined with the concept of containerization. (Doug Grieve Collection)

aimed at reducing costs. One of the most significant developments of this decade was the introduction of hauling two trailers at one time, commonly referred to as 'doubles.' By the mid-1960s, three 27-foot (8.2m) trailers rather than two 40-foot (12m) trailers were becoming popular.

Piggybacking was also on the increase, and by 1962 over 25,000 trailers had been built. As the decade went on, Piggybacking – combined with the concept of 'containerization' that first appeared in the 1950s – proved to be a boon to both the railroad and trucking business. Piggybacking was fast and far less expensive, while containerization proved ideal for the transport and interchange between ships and aircraft.

In 1969m a fibreglass air shield mounted on the roof of the truck cab was introduced by Rudkin-Wiley Corporation to reduce drag by deflecting air up and over and around the trailer. The concept would eventually be used throughout the industry to reduce fuel consumption.

Any concept that would reduce fuel consumption and costs was considered worthwhile. The fibreglass air shield mounted on the roof of the truck cab, first introduced by the Rudkin-Wiley Corporation in 1969 to reduce drag, was soon a standard fitting in the 1970s. (Doug Grieve Collection)

Another way trucking firms found they could reduce costs was through leasing. Throughout the 1960s the full-service or short-term rental truck leasing industry grew in popularity.

There were also many material usage breakthroughs in trailer construction and design, particularly with refrigeration and insulation methods. In the same vein, air-conditioned truck cabs became more popular, and were noted as being a contributing factor to safety.

This decade also saw the further development of air compression brakes, as well as other brake and speed reduction systems such as anti-lock braking. Emergency braking and anti-skid systems were also being developed by the end of the 1960s.

By 1969 the trucks, the industry, and North America itself were very different from just a decade before. Sales soared; the truck manufacturers that had survived the decade were building nearly two million units.

● CONTAINERIZATION

A method of freight handling developed for maximum utilization of facilities of shipper, receiver and carrier to eliminate costly handling or delay of power units.

Equipment has been planned and engineered to permit lowest possible operating cost and maximum efficiency.

Consult our nearest Branch Office for full particulars.

The concept of containerization first appeared in the 1950s. Piggybacking and containerization were a boon to both railroad and trucking businesses, in terms of speed and cost. (Doug Grieve Collection)

Throughout the 1960s the full-service or short-term rental truck leasing industry grew in popularity. Companies such as Hertz developed large fleets to meet the increasing demand. (Doug Grieve Collection)

Air conditioned truck cabs became increasingly popular. At first, the air conditioning unit was roof-mounted and thus open to the elements. This led to increased fuel costs and proved unreliable at first, while the hole cut in the roof often meant leaks and drafts. (Doug Grieve Collection)

Throughout the decade braking systems steadily improved, making trucks safer, as well as providing the stopping power necessary for hauling heavier loads, doubles, and, eventually, triple trailers. (Andrew Mort)

Delivering on time – American truck companies and models of the 1960s

Autocar

As one of the earliest vehicle manufacturers in the United States, dating back to 1897, Autocar was a very saleable nameplate with a long history of building reliable trucks.

Following WWII, it suffered financial setbacks due to a general industry-wide slowdown. By 1953, with million dollar losses mounting, Autocar was taken over by the White Motor Corporation. Although rationalisation in designs and powertrains took place, White continued production, making Autocars the top-of-the-line models. The Autocar division of White focused on larger, heavier trucks, and, in the late 1950s, Autocar developed its 'AP' series of on-off highway trucks. The largest was the 600hp V12 diesel engine AP40, capable of hauling a payload capacity of 40 tons (36,280kg) with a substantially larger GCW. The A-series first appeared in 1958 and featured a lightweight aluminium chassis, which reduced the overall weight by 25 per cent and thus increased the payload by 2.25 tons.

In 1960, Autocar was also building the C models available with a stainless steel cab. Both diesel and White's gasoline engine were offered, but in the 1960s 6-cylinder diesels from Cummins, Detroit Diesel, and Caterpillar became the most popular powerplant choices. Interestingly, by the mid-1960s, a gasoline engine was no longer offered in an Autocar.

White continued to build Autocar trucks powered by its own line of engines, as well as offer the new-in-1962 DCV heavy-duty series powered by Cummins V8-265 diesel engines. Eventually purchased by GMC/AB Volvo, the Autocar nameplate continued in production until 2000. Ultimately sold to Grand Vehicle Works Ltd in 2001, this firm then introduced a low COE truck, known as the Autocar Xpeditor, primarily for use in the refuse industry. Interestingly, the 'Xpeditor' nameplate was previously a model offered by White. A DCV-powered White with a fibreglass hood is pictured. (Doug Grieve Collection)

Autocar's range during the 1960s became more focused on use in all aspects of the construction and aircraft industries. However, it continued to build a truck to meet the customer's specific needs in conventional, COE and half-cab design.

White put Autocar in charge of its experimental turbine engine project, but, like everyone else's foray into this modern powerplant, it was eventually dropped. The 600hp engine utilised was built by the Orenda Division of Hawker-Siddeley Canada Ltd.

As the decade ended Autocar's future appeared bright, and the nameplate would continue to survive right into the millennium.

In the 1960s Autocar built 4x2, 4x4, 6x4 and 8x4 haulers. Pictured is a 6x4 DC10364S powered by a 280hp diesel engine utilising the Autocar Driver Cab that was first introduced in 1950, and continued in production until 1987. This particular DC was built for export to Australia. (Doug Grieve Collection)

The Autocar truck line-up in the 1960s ranged from a 23-ton (20,866kg) GVW to a 100-ton (90,720kg) GVW. The Autocar line of cement mixers featured a custom heavy-duty design, and was offered in 6x4, 8x4, 6x6, and 6x8 models. Pictured here is an Autocar DC9364 diesel-powered 6x8 with a 50,000lb (22,608kg) capacity rear axle and 18,000lb (8165kg) front axle. (Doug Grieve Collection)

Autocar's range during the 1960s became more focused on the construction and aircraft industries. Autocar also continued building trucks to meet customers' specific needs in conventional, COE, and even half-cab design for highway use. (Doug Grieve Collection)

Autocar's AP25 was a heavy-duty model powered by a 434hp V12 Detroit Diesel. (Doug Grieve Collection)

Brockway

New York State-based Brockway dated back to 1912, but, like many firms, it was in a dire financial state in the early 1950s. As a result, Brockway became a division of Mack in 1956, but continued to design its own range under the 'Huskie' name, which appeared in 1958.

The first Brockway truck to bear the Huskie nameplate was the Model 258. Brockway also continued to supply chassis to various companies that built fire trucks. By 1961 the Huskie nameplate and styling cues were being applied to the lighter trucks in the Brockway line-up.

With fourteen 125hp to 230hp gas-powered models being offered by 1961, Brockway trucks continued to be a familiar sight in North America. Introduced that year was the upgraded Model 158 powered by a 200hp, 458ci (7.5-litre) Continental engine. With its traditional folding hood on both sides, and easily removable (set-aside) front fenders, the Huskie was easier to maintain than some of the competition.

In 1963 Brockway built its first COE/BBC Huskie. Known as the 400-series, it was based on the Mack F-series that had been successfully introduced a year earlier.

As the 1960s went on, Brockway trucks were being offered with the familiar Continental gas engine, or the optional Cummins or Detroit Diesel engines. By 1965 the Continental had disappeared, but a Caterpillar engine was soon added to the now all-diesel line-up.

A new 300-series appeared in 1965, as did a V8 diesel engine along with the 855ci (14-litre) NH-250 Cummins 6-cylinder diesel.

Other drivetrain changes that followed included the

The 'Huskie' radiator mascot became the symbol of Brockway trucks just as the Mack 'Bulldog' had become the trademark of the parent company decades before.
(Doug Grieve Collection)

Brockway celebrated its Golden Anniversary in 1962. These trucks were identified by a 'gold' emblem and 'Huskie' hood ornament rather than chrome. (Doug Grieve Collection)

Brockway's first COE/BBC design Huskie was based on the Mack F-series, and was introduced in 1963 as the 400-series. (Doug Grieve Collection)

Fifty different models in the 300-series Brockway trucks were introduced in 1965, available in either conventional or COE designs. (Doug Grieve Collection)

The Huskiedrive five-speed transmission with a two-speed axle in 1968 for its Cummins NHCT Custom Torque, diesel-powered, heavy-duty trucks. With the Huskiedrive you simply flicked a switch on the dash to " ... attain cruising speed and increase horsepower, while simultaneously improving fuel economy and extending truck life." As well, "Huskiedrive permits you to cruise in the ideal operating range of 1800rpm where the engine develops 248hp." These models were easily identified by the twin huskie hood ornaments. (Doug Grieve Collection)

introduction of the 'Huskiedrive' 5-speed transmission with a 2-speed axle in 1968. An 8-speed was later offered.

Brockway trucks eventually disappeared in 1977 when the plant was shut down by Mack, more due to the parent company's financial difficulties and costs involved in meeting new industry safety and pollution regulations than poor sales.

In 1960, all Chevrolet trucks featured a fresh chassis design to increase ride comfort, load-handling, and safety, as well as fresh styling inside and out. Chevrolet truck production rose 21 per cent in 1960, including pickup trucks, while the entire trucking industry saw only a 5 per cent increase. (Doug Grieve Collection)

Chevrolet

Chevrolet trucks first appeared in 1918 and proved to be very popular over the ensuing decades. A full range of models was developed from a great deal of sharing – and ultimately duplicating – with General Motor's official truck subsidiary GMC.

By 1958 the styling bore the common characteristics of both Chevrolet's cars and its smaller pickup truck line-up. Dual headlamps, full air brakes, and larger V8 engines were also being offered in its big truck models. This family resemblance continued through the entire Chevrolet line, and was even evident amidst the radical changes that took place in 1960. In appearance the all-new Chevrolet trucks were different inside and out. The emphasis was on style and comfort, and these new trucks had both. Also, the chassis

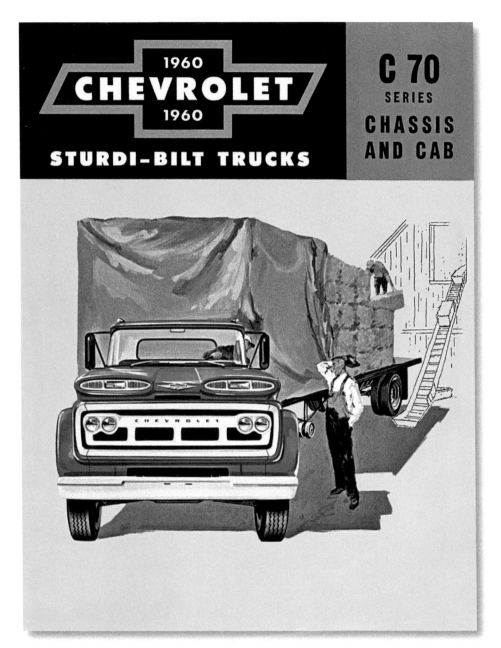

1960
CHEVROLET
1960

STURDI-BILT TRUCKS

C 70
SERIES

CHASSIS AND CAB

was completely reworked with new frames and steering boxes. The conventionals all got independent front suspensions with torsion bars, while the rear suspension was redesigned, and featured standard variable leaf springs on the Chevy medium and heavy-duty trucks.

The model designations were also all changed in 1960. The heavy-duty models were known as the Spartan line. The conventional models all started with a C, the cab forward models were P, the low cab forwards were L, the tandem units were M, and the tilt-cabs were T. The first digit referred to tonnage, the second wheelbase length, and the last two body style. One popular powerplant was the 230hp, 348ci (5.7-litre) gasoline V8.

CHEVROLET'S BIG PAYLOAD L.C.F.'S FOR '60

In 1961 GMC and Chevrolet models shared most designs, except for the Chevrolet LCF model which was not available as a GMC truck. (Doug Grieve Collection)

The new BBC class tilt-cab trucks appeared late in the 1960 model year, and featured torsion bar ride on their independent front suspension.

Few changes occurred in 1961, other than an increase in the GVW rating to 51,000 pounds (23,134kg) on all its heavy-duty models.

Chevrolet offered the largest truck line-up in its history in 1962 with 203 different models, but only ten were medium-duty and ten others heavy-duty trucks. Twenty new diesel models were offered in the 60- and 80-series. (The 70-series was dropped, and the tandem model became the M80.) Chevrolet began dropping its dual headlamp design that year, although it was still evident on the tilt-cab. While the new and larger

The 1962 LCF E80-series was the first heavy-duty GMC model (B-series). Fundamentally, all that was required for it to become a Chevrolet was a change in badges. It was powered by the GM-built 195hp, 2-cycle, 318ci (5.2L) diesel engine. The 8 millionth Chevrolet truck was built in 1962. (Doug Grieve Collection)

Chevrolet offered a T-series (for tilt-cab), which was virtually identical to the U-series version powered by a diesel engine. (Doug Grieve Collection)

409ci (6.7-litre) gasoline V8 was optional on the M80, Chevrolet was aware of the emerging trend toward diesel engines, and released two GM-built 6-cylinder units. Still, the Division's largest 6x4 heavy-duty trucks were powered by 195hp V6 Detroit Diesel engines.

The Chevrolet tilt-cab model remained popular in both the medium-duty and heavy-duty line-up. In heavy-duty guise it was offered with either gas or diesel power.

Only 178 models were offered in 1963, and a redesigned body led to a decrease in overall width which increased manoeuverability. All the frames were likewise changed, and the independent front suspension on its medium- and heavy-duty trucks was dropped.

In 1964, Chevrolet once again expanded its line-up with a new diesel-powered tandem axle model, designated the W80, which in appearance looked like the E80 trucks already being produced.

Chevrolet's truck line-up surged to 324 models in 1965, and although it would be the last year for the A60, A80, E80 and spin-off BBC models, the range

The new 1969 Chevrolet Titan could be ordered with a variety of engines, including a Detroit Diesel V6, V8 or V12, or Cummins diesels. As well as having up to 475hp, the Titan featured dual disc clutches, a ten- or thirteen-speed transmission, power steering, and air brakes and suspension. (Doug Grieve Collection)

1966 saw the introduction of the tilt-cab 70,000- and 80,000-series, in either single or tandem axle form. These more aerodynamic models were offered with two new gas engines; the GMC 401ci (6.6L) V6, and the 478 (7.8L) V6, as well as two diesels. Pictured are (top-to-bottom): the HG70000, HV70000, and HJ70000. (Doug Grieve Collection)

grew by another 42 models in 1966. Out of that total there were 101 new heavy-duty Series 70,000 and 80,000 trucks in conventional and COE versions.

In 1967 the medium-duty 40, 50, 60-series received shorter wheelbases and new cabs, but only minor modifications and specification changes were made to the heavy-duty range. Similar updates and changes continued into 1968, and sales increased. This was reflected throughout the entire industry, with a record breaking 1,950,713 trucks sold.

As the decade ended Chevrolet introduced its largest truck line to date: the tilt-cab 4x2 and 6x4 Titan. With its aluminium cab, this tractor trailer had a GCW of 65,000lb (29,484kg).

Challenge-Cook to 1964

The Cook Brothers Equipment Company of Los Angeles, California prospered during the first half of the 1950s, building trucks for the West Coast, but it was absorbed by another company later in the decade and became known as Challenge-Cook. Challenge Manufacturing built cement mixers and Cook supplied the chassis. Interestingly, Cook was unique in that it continued to use chain-drive right into the early 1960s. Other chassis were also supplied, but, by 1964, Cook as a nameplate disappeared.

Diamond T – to 1967

Diamond T trucks first appeared in 1911 and the firm soon established a name for quality and reliability. In fact, in 1940 Diamond T became the first trucking company to introduce a 100,000 mile (160,000km) or one year guarantee on all its trucks.

Following WWII the company continued to prosper, in part due to military contracts, but stiff competition and the changing times resulted in White buying financially strapped Diamond T in 1958. By 1960 production of Diamond T (Chicago) and previously purchased REO was now being carried out in the REO plant in Lancing, Michigan. Diamond T retained its identity as a separate make, but utilised REO, White, Autocar, and other subsidiary engines, cabs, and components.

In that year, production commenced of the new R cab, Diamond T 5000-series, and two new V8

The new Diamond T Model 931C COE, with a BBC of only 50 inches, was introduced in 1961, and offered with optional engine choices ranging from four gas-powered 6-cylinders, or two V8s, to five Cummins 6-cylinder diesels, including the super-charged 262hp, 69sci NTO-6. The model pictured is from 1963. (Doug Grieve Collection)

Diamond T introduced the Model 534CG, 634CG and 734CG in 1960, featuring a fibreglass cab which, reportedly, reduced cab weight by 360lb (163kg). Pictured is a later Diamond REO version. (Doug Grieve Collection)

engines known as the DT8-207 and the DT8-235 with the numerical designation signifying the horsepower. Although treated as separate entities under the same roof, both REO and Diamond T utilised the White/REO conventional D and R cabs. A fibreglass, manual tilt-cab was used on the various 500 through 800 models. Diesel and gas straight six, V6 and V8 engines were offered, as well as GM's 4-cylinder diesel engine.

1961 saw the introduction of the new model 931C COE, and model line-up was further enhanced in 1963 with the announcement of the diesel-powered P2000D, the P3000D (fitted with the R cab from REO, first seen in 1939), and the 533CG.

An Autocar was the basis of the new 1000 model introduced in 1966, nicknamed the Westerner. Also unveiled at this time was – according to Diamond T – a trendsetting design in the form of a 'synthetic steel' (plastic-like) cab.

The Diamond T Model 990 featured the Autocar 'D' cab, and was the basis of the new Air-Flo 931C unveiled in 1962. It sported two curved sections on its front windscreen that improved aerodynamics and increased visibility. (Doug Grieve Collection)

DIAMOND *featuring* **T**rend **HF-3000**

The Diamond T Trend cab features a manual spring loaded tilt feature. Tilting takes only a few seconds and is easily handled by the driver alone. Accessibility is outstanding, with the entire power train exposed for servicing. This means ease of service, and therefore, lower maintenance and labor costs.

LONG LIFE

TILT CAB DESIGN

HIGH MANEUVERABILITY

LOW OPERATING AND MAINTENANCE COSTS

1966 saw the unveiling of the Diamond T 'Lifetime Cab' known as the 'Trend.' Made of Royalex plastic material, it featured a steel and aluminium framework and galvanized steel doors. The driver sat atop the engine in this COE, providing a flat floor. Diamond T also noted it was one of the easiest to work tilt-cab designs on the market. (Doug Grieve Collection)

CF-6842 SERIES **TREND**®
WITH "LIFE TIME" CAB

CF-6842

DIAMOND REO

**Leader in its class
for economy... efficiency!**

Diamond REO originally offered the impressive 'Trend' with a 185hp, 327ci gasoline V8, and later a 235hp V8, as well as various diesel engines. There were four models in the 1968 line-up: the 240, 255, 260 and 275, with each reflecting the GVW rating (ie 240 being 24,000lb (10,887kg), the 255 being 25,500lb (11,567kg), etc). (Doug Grieve Collection)

Diamond REO from 1967

In 1967, White combined its REO and Diamond T product line to become the Diamond REO Division. (In the first half of the 1970s White would divest itself of the Diamond REO Division.)

C-114

DIAMOND REO

This Diamond REO conventional C-114 Series was powered by a choice of diesel engines, ranging from 190-335hp. (Doug Grieve Collection)

Initially thirty models were offered – virtually all the former models, but these were given fresh designations. Advertising at the time boasted, "You can practically 'design' your own new Diamond REO ... and we'll build it for you. It's just like ordering a tailor-made suit instead of picking one off the rack." During this time combinations of steel, aluminium, fibreglass and plastic cabs were offered.

Diamond T's Trend cab was offered by all the White-owned lines including its farm divisions Oliver and Minneapolis-Moline. The Trend body was now supplied by Uniroyal Synthetic Steel following acquisitions and mergers. Some Diamond REO military trucks were built in 1968, but no other contracts came along again until 1972.

Dodge's LCF C-series trucks introduced in 1960 came in a full range, with the smallest being a 5-ton with a choice of straight 6 and V8 engines. The largest C-series featured a GVW of over 12 tons (24,000kg) hauled by a Cummins diesel engine. Dodge was now in the heavy-duty, diesel truck business. 'Servi-Swing' front fenders swung out 110 degrees for easy, walk-in engine maintenance. The swing-out fender could act as a temporary place for tools, on a specially-designed inner shelf, or hold the entire weight of a mechanic if necessary. (Doug Grieve Collection)

Dodge

The Dodge brothers began building trucks in Detroit in 1916, but in 1927 the firm was purchased by Walter P Chrysler to become the Dodge Division of Chrysler Corporation. Dodge trucks were built throughout the 1930s and '40s, and from 1943-45 alone it built over 500,000 military trucks.

Commercial truck production continued after the war, with the largest Dodge trucks in 1959 being the D-900 and T-900 powered by the 234hp Hemi V8.

The Dodge-cloned Fargo trucks also continued to be built and offered in Canada, as well as for export, while DeSoto trucks were built for export only.

1960 saw the discontinuation of Dodge's COE models and the introduction of a new C-series of LCF (low cab forward) medium and heavy-duty trucks

A Dodge 1000 diesel in a press photo demonstrating great pulling power. (Chrysler Corporation)

DODGE
BUILDS
TOUGH
TRUCKS

1962

MEDIUM-TONNAGE MODELS				
	D-400	D-500	D-600	D-700
CAB-FORWARD		C-500	C-600	C-700
MAX GVW. LBS.	15,000	19,500	22,000	25,000
MAX GCW. LBS.	25,000	34,000	36,000	50,000

A minor facelift for Dodge's D-series resulted in a substantial increase in sales in 1962, as buyers approved of the new, bolder styling. Dodge also extended its gas-powered, heavy-duty truck warranty to 100,000 miles (160,930km), and adopted a new policy of foregoing annual model changes in favour of making upgrades and improvements on a regular basis. (Doug Grieve Collection)

powered by a choice of either gas or newly offered diesel engines. The LCF design was an alternative to conventionals and the more expensive COE models. The C-series included 6x4 models up to 26.5 tons (24,041kg). The D-series continued to be popular, particularly as a medium-duty truck, and was a regular best-seller in the line-up. The medium-duty D models were joined in 1960 by a P-series based on the LCF design, and the 4x4 W-series continued in production.

The truck line-up was further expanded in 1962 with more optional diesel engines from Cummins and Perkins.

The Dodge L-series COE was introduced in 1964. It was one of Dodge's last attempts to become a major manufacturer in the big truck field. (Doug Grieve Collection)

In 1964 Dodge offered COE versions known as the L-series, which remained in production until 1974.

Dodge confirmed its commitment in the heavy-duty truck market by opening a new designated plant in Warren, Michigan in 1966 capable of building a dozen LCF and LN1000 diesel trucks an hour. This plant offered more diesel engine options, and soon Detroit Diesel and Caterpillar units were also being fitted into heavy-duty Dodge trucks. About a year later the plant was expanded to meet demand.

The medium-duty L600 COE utilised the compact A-100 pickup truck cab, and was offered as a straight truck or in tractor form. The L600 had a GCW of 18 tons (16,330kg), while the larger L700 was rated at a GCW of 25 tons (22,680kg). Standard power in the L700 was a 360ci V8, but in the L600 a Perkins diesel was offered as an optional engine. (Doug Grieve Collection)

A new medium-duty COE truck joined the line-up in 1966, utilising the compact A-100 pickup truck cab.

The long running W-series trucks ceased to be offered in 1969 in the commercial market, although Dodge built them well into the 1970s for military use.

Despite the company's success in the 1960s, Dodge found the competition fierce in the heavy truck market, and in 1975 closed its operations to concentrate on light-duty trucks. The Fargo nameplate was officially dropped in Canada in 1972, but continued to be used by Chrysler in other parts of the world.

Dodge also built the P-series 'Forward Control Vans' with GVW ratings in the 5400-16,000lb range.
(Doug Grieve Collection)

W500 POWER WAGON

The W-series trucks were first introduced during WWII with the last big changes occurring in 1961. This version of the W-series was offered on the commercial market until 1969. Due to demand, Dodge continued to build the W-series well into the 1970s for the US military. (Doug Grieve Collection)

The Fargo nameplate was popular in Canada and known around the world. It disappeared in Canada in 1972. Interestingly, this 1968 Fargo 900 was never licensed for the road, as it was used on a college campus only. (Andrew Mort)

The Ford C-series became the longest-running, production-built truck to date. Beginning in the 1950s, it was sold throughout the 1960s and 1970s and into the early 1980s. (Doug Grieve Collection)

Ford

In 1957, the new 1957 C-series COE was introduced. This version continued in concept right into the 1990s, and would be copied by many in the industry with its cab hinged at the front to tilt forward for drivetrain access.

By 1959 Ford's model choices had expanded to 370 with the arrival of the first factory-built, four-wheel-drive vehicles. Ford continued to expand its highly successful truck line-up in the new decade by offering 488 different models.

Ford's T-series ('T for tandem) continued to be offered throughout the decade. (Doug Grieve Collection)

In 1960 Ford began developing a gas-turbine-powered truck, eventually known as 'Big Red.' Pictured here at Ford world headquarters is a very young Doug Grieve. By the end of the decade Ford had abandoned the project. (Doug Grieve Collection)

When the '60s began, Ford was offering its C-series COE models, its medium-duty versions of the F-series, as well as its T-series.

As part of the 619 model line-up in 1961, Ford introduced its then mega-sized H-series high-built, tilt-cab tractors for interstate use. That year also marked the introduction of the first Ford truck powered by a diesel engine.

With up to 12 speeds, Ford's top-of-the-line H-series tractor models in 4x2 and 4x6 form were offered in 1961 with a choice of 401, 477 or 534ci gas-powered V8 engines, as well as with an option of five Cummins diesels for the largest models in the range. An unbelievable five hundred different engine/transmission/axle combinations were available. (Andrew Mort)

The F-series continued to be a popular choice in the medium-duty range, and was given a facelift and a 1in (2.5cm) increase in headroom, as were the T- and N-series conventionals in 1964. However, in 1966 Ford added another 3.5in (9cm) to the headroom in all these trucks. Note the aftermarket sleeper. (Doug Grieve Collection)

Ford's new W-series was unveiled in 1965. This new line of boxy, steel, high-tilt COE models were powered by diesel engines and offered in a staggering 1250 different forms. (Doug Grieve Collection)

Appearing in 1963 was Ford's N-series, powered by either a gas or diesel engine. This short-hood, high-rise conventional design provided the N with a distinctive appearance. The cab was based on the F-series, but pushed further forward. It was a less expensive alternative to the H-series, and was offered in medium-, heavy- and super heavy-duty guises. (Doug Grieve Collection)

Ford continued to expand its truck line-up both big and small. Ford built over 375,000 trucks (including vans, pickups, SUVs, and buses) in 1962, and by 1963 was offering over 1000 individual models. Not surprisingly, the total reached 563,137 Ford Trucks in 1965.

In 1966 Ford replaced its H-series COE with a new W-series.

Ford was now using more and more proprietary engines in its trucks, and began offering Detroit Diesels in its F/T-8000 and new N/NT-8000 models.

On a corporate level Ford formed a special Motor Truck Operations division in 1968, and set up a nationwide network of new Ford Truck Centres for exclusive sale and service of its medium and heavy-duty truck models. (The corporate title would be re-named the Truck and Recreation Product Operations in 1972.)

As it had at the close of the previous decade, Ford continued to chase General Motors to lead the industry in truck sales despite selling over 640,000 units. The future looked bright in the trucking industry, and by 1970 Ford had opened its new Louisville line. Even more Ford trucks began to roll out of the world's largest factory devoted exclusively to trucks.

Freightliner production rose every year except in 1967 when it dipped slightly. Still, from a meager 903 trucks built in 1960 it boasted a production of 8674 units in 1969, thanks in part to its COE design dating back to 1958. Pictured is a White Freightliner. (Courtesy Freightliner)

Freightliner

Leland James founded Freightliner Corporation in Salt Lake City on August 19th, 1942. Despite severe setbacks, by 1951 the company had established a fine reputation in the industry – so much so that White signed an agreement to create White-Freightliner, to sell and service Freightliner trucks through White dealerships. This allowed Freightliner to concentrate on design and production. Over the next 25 years Freightliner sold over 100,000 trucks through White dealerships in the US and Canada.

In the latter half of 1958, Freightliner introduced the industry's first full 90-degree, tilt-cab COE, and sales increased 33 per cent.

Buoyed by this success in the marketplace,

Freightliner continued to expand in the 1960s. A new production plant opened in Los Angeles County, a national parts distribution warehouse in Chicago, and production began in Canada. By 1961, production had reached 1242 units annually.

In 1965, the experimental TurboLiner with a gas-turbine engine appeared in co-operation with Boeing and Caterpillar. Although it weighed 2400lb less than comparable piston-driven rigs, the rising cost of gasoline doomed the project. Despite this disappointment, sales reached 4786 units – up 30 per cent over 1964 totals. Further successes and expansion over the decade saw production top 11,000 units annually by 1972, and, by October 1974, the 100,000th Freightliner had rolled off the assembly line.

FWD Corporation introduced a new Tractioneer series in 1962, featuring either rear or multi-drive versions. An innovation was the electronically operated 'Traction Lock' drivetrain, activated with a flick of a switch on the dash. *(Doug Grieve Collection)*

FWD

FWD took its name from its original 1910 car and truck design of 'four-wheel-drive,' and was officially founded in Clintonville, Wisconsin in 1912. FWD became the FWD Corporation in 1960. It was a heavy-duty specialist company building vehicles for the oil fields, utilities and logging industries, fire fighting, construction companies, road maintenance, crane carriers and the military. FWD's specialised trucks included vehicles with multi-axles and 8x8 configurations throughout the 1960s. In 1963,

FWD also introduced its ForWarD Mover COE in 1968, which featured a reverse-sloping 'control tower' windscreen, a setback front axle, and a 138in wheelbase. (Doug Grieve Collection)

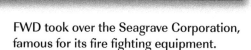

A new FWD heavy-duty conventional tractor model appeared in 1968. It was the first FWD truck that was 2WD. (Doug Grieve Collection)

FWD took over the Seagrave Corporation, famous for its fire fighting equipment.

GMC

The General Motors Truck Company was established in 1911, and, by the time the auto show took place in 1912, the make had officially become known as GMC. GMC quickly became a leader in the US trucking industry, and by 1958 was marketing a line of trucks ranging from a ½-ton (454kg) to 45-ton (40,815kg) 8000 series. GMC had captured over seven percent of the total truck market in the US as the decade drew to a close.

For its completely new 1960 truck model range, GMC announced a new line of V6 engines and a 275hp V12. By 1960, GMC was one of the largest builders of trucks in the United States. Apart from its bus chassis and smaller light-duty and pickup trucks, GMC built twenty B conventionals, sixteen

New V-6 Engine—Today's only modern truck power!

CROSS SECTIONS THROUGH GMC MODEL 401 V-6 ENGINE

GMC built 104,310 trucks in 1960. Its new engines and C and L Series led the way. Pictured is a C60-series gasoline tanker truck. (Andrew Mort)

Fitted as standard in its 1960 line, GMC announced its BW5500 and BW5500 tandem axle trucks and tractors. and L6000 and L6000 trucks and tractors powered by the new GMC V6 gasoline engine. Rated at 205hp, this 400.9ci motor featured seventy-three interchangeable parts within all GMC V6 engines. to provide greater parts availability and standardisation.
(Author's collection)

41

Twin-Six Gasoline Engine

KING OF GMC's NEW
GASOLINE ENGINE
FAMILY . . .

702—"B" Conventional Models

702—Tilt cab Models

GMC 702 ENGINE

Max. gross B.H.P. ....275 @ 2400 r.p.m.
Max. net B.H.P. ....250 @ 2400 r.p.m.
Max. gross torque (lbs.ft.) ....630 @ 1600-1900 r.p.m.
Max. net torque (lbs.ft.) ....585 @ 1600-1800 r.p.m.
Bore, 4.56 in. ....Stroke, 3.58 in.
Displacement. ....702.4 cu. in.
Compression ratio. ....7.50 to 1

The new GMC twin six 702ci gasoline engine, introduced in 1960, had a gross bhp of 275@2400rpm. (Author's collection)

This fleet of LW7000 GMC trucks was owned by Kingsway Transport in Ontario, Canada. These COE models were powered by GMC's 702 twin 6-cylinder engine rated at 275hp. (Doug Grieve Collection)

In 1962 GMC launched the D-series COE which was nicknamed the 'Crackerbox' due to its tall, thin, rectangular looks. The engine was most often a Detroit Diesel. Pictured is a 1966 model. (Andrew Mort)

gas-powered tilt-cabs, two forward cab models, ten B diesel-powered conventionals, five diesel tilt-cab and eight BBC tilt-cab models. There was an equally impressive engine line-up, with a choice of ten gas or diesel motors.

Altogether in 1960 GMC offered a total of sixty-one different models, designated from 1000 to 9000, and ranging from a ½-ton (454kg) to 60-ton (54432kg) truck. Interestingly, GMC offered one straight 6-cylinder gas or diesel engine, a choice of five V6 gas engines, and two versions of its diesel V6, but there was initially no V8 engine in the 1960 line-up.

GM's Diesel Motor Division supplied both GMC and sister division Chevrolet with twelve multifuel engines that ran on everything from gasoline to diesel fuel.

The Diesel Motor Division also offered conversion kits for customers to change existing diesel engines to multifuel. In its larger trucks, GMC basically offered a choice of nine different engines, including a new Detroit Diesel 2-stroke V8 in some of its 7100 and 8100 D-series models.

As well as fresh and upgraded engines, the styling and chassis design was all-new for 1960. Chassis upgrades included IFS on the GMC medium-size trucks and air suspension on the bigger models. All these changes were promoted in a huge GMC advertising campaign. There was a redesigned 72in tall, 78in wide, BBC COE tilt, featuring the new independent front wheel torsion-spring suspension with a GVW of 19,500lb (8845kg), and capable of hauling 60 tons (54,432kg), and V12 models fitted with a twin clutch, 10-speed transmission and air brakes. Production in 1960 would increase by over 25,000 units to 104,310 commercial vehicles.

In 1961 you could choose from a GMC 48in, all aluminium tilt-cab, to a 90-inch all-steel conventional. It was all personal choice. The 4000-series, for example, presented the shipper with a choice of 34 different engine/transmission/axle combinations to fit the company's professional needs.

In 1963 GMC revised its chassis design by switching from its I-section rails to the more industry standard channel side-members, and abandoning its independent front suspension and air suspension systems.

The V12 was offered until 1964, when GMC finally switched from 2-stroke to 4-stroke diesels, although 2-stroke diesels were still offered. The most powerful engine in this line-up became the first-ever GMC diesel-powered, 4-stroke V8. The Torq-Flow 220bhp diesel engine was part of the new Magnum series. Magnum V6 engines were also available.

By the mid-sixties GMC also offered a full range of 8, 10 and 16-speed transmissions, and in 1966 the line-up consisted of 102 basic models of trucks that were further offered with a multitude of engine/transmission/axle and chassis possibilities.

The big news in 1967 was the GMC takeover from Chevrolet of all medium- and heavy-duty truck design

GMC's new 1969 Astro 95 COE featured new service and repair features that reduced maintenance time and costs. The aluminium cab was only partly welded, with some panels pop-riveted for easy replacement. The cab could also be tilted to 45 degrees or to a full vertical position for engine access. Additionally, the Astro had colour-keyed wiring, routed and mounted along the frame rails for quick repair.
(Doug Grieve Collection)

and production, although both badges were still used. In fact, Chevrolet added the H-series conventionals to its line-up as well as a new E-series, and in 1968 a 260bhp, 427ci V8 engine was offered that ran on regular gas.

As the decade ended, GMC introduced the Astro 95, which featured an all-aluminium tilt-cab. It incorporated many new features for faster servicing and repairs.

By 1969 GMC was building a record-breaking 150,180 heavy-duty units.

The Canada-built Hayes Clipper was available as a COE.
This is a 1966 version. (Norman Wood Collection)

Hayes

The Canadian-based Hayes trucks date back to 1928. After focusing on conversions and building trucks for the logging industry and dock work, Hayes began building its own trucks. Following WWII, Hayes introduced a new line of highway tractors powered by Detroit Diesel, Leyland, Cummins, Caterpillar, and even Rolls-Royce engines.

Throughout the 1960s Hayes offered highway trucks in conventional and COE models, but it always remained focused on the logging industry, and built trucks capable of hauling up to 150 tons (136,080kg).

Always a low volume, specialist company, the final new Hayes tractor trailer unit was the latest evolutionary conventional in the Clipper line, and was known as the 200. In 1969, the standard engine was the popular Cummins NH-200 diesel engine, although thirteen other possible powerplants were offered to customers.

Production was limited, and in 1969 Mack became a major stockholder. Hayes was eventually purchased by PACCAR in 1974, and the nameplate disappeared shortly thereafter.

The Hayes Clipper was also available as a conventional. Hayes was a solely Canadian-owned company, the oldest and largest truck manufacturing company in the country.
(Doug Grieve Collection)

During the 1960s Hendrickson built trucks for fleet use, but specialised in custom-built, super heavy-weight trucks such as this giant. (Doug Grieve Collection)

Hendrickson

Magnus Hendrickson and his sons established their own Hendrickson Motor Truck Company in 1913. In 1948, the Mobile Equipment Division took over the building of conventional Hendrickson trucks utilising International K-series cabs. In the 1950s Hendrickson specialised in custom-built, heavy-duty and super heavy-weight trucks for 200 tons (181,400kg) and more, as well as highway trucks and tractors.

Over the decade, these special super heavy-weight chassis designs were purchased by other manufacturers.

Throughout the 1960s, Hendrickson built refuse trucks, a B-series truck appropriately named 'Pinocchio Nose,' and a tilt-cab tractor. Further special super heavy-weight trucks were built for the military, but the largest appeared in the latter half of the 1960s to transport hydro-electric transformers to Churchill Falls in Labrador, Canada. It had a GCW of 1,250,000lb (567,000kg).

In 1960 International added a compact diesel tractor, designated the BC-225D, as a four- or six-wheel that featured a chassis utilising a great deal of weight-saving aluminium. (Doug Grieve Collection)

International

International Harvester had a long, proud history in building trucks, heavy equipment, tractors, etc, dating back to early 1900s high-wheelers.

The founders behind International were Cyrus H McCormick, Henry Weber and William Deering who began manufacturing farm equipment and wagons in the mid-19th century. The firm became a leader in farm equipment and continued to develop its truck manufacturing. By 1957, International was celebrating its Golden Anniversary in the trucking business.

The GVW of the new M-series and F230 of 1962 were up to 78,000lb (35,381kg). (Doug Grieve Collection)

That same year it introduced the A series, AC and ACO. This was followed in 1959 by a B and BC series. These trucks helped push International to the forefront of the trucking industry. From 1950-1959, production reached more than 1,283,000 units, including school buses, military vehicles, construction vehicles, etc.

In 1961, International launched its new C-series line of pickups and wagons, which interestingly utilised the B-series cab, but sitting lower into the frame.

The International offered ideal 50/50 weight distribution and a choice of optional Detroit Diesel or Cummins diesel engines.
(Doug Grieve Collection)

In 1965 International introduced its D-series. Pictured is a 2000D, diesel-powered example. (Doug Grieve Collection)

This 1966 Loadstar 1600 conventional was owned and operated by William Grieve of Toronto, father of contributor Doug Grieve. (Doug Grieve Collection)

Also appearing in 1965 was the wider CO-4000 COE models, in anticipation of changes in the law regarding width. (Doug Grieve Collection)

Late 1961, International announced its medium and light-duty Loadstar trucks with a standard 193hp, 304ci V8. A diesel engine was optional. The Loadstar line was sold alongside the B-series until 1967.

In 1962, International added a new series to its bigger truck lines, with its conventional M-series and F230 models designed for the construction industry. International also began supplying the construction industry with 2x4 and 4x4 dump trucks with a GVW of up to 154,000lb (69,854kg). The new International Payhauler dump truck of 1964 was the industry's first 4x4, with dual tires front and rear.

International continued to unveil new models, but also kept moving away from the traditional use of letters and numbers, instead

International's line-up expanded in both the larger and smaller range (which included the 1300-series). Pictured here is a 1966 version. (Andrew Mort)

The Fleetstar was introduced in 1968 to replace the ageing R-series that had been introduced in 1953. The Fleetstar cab was mounted to the frame via coil springs. (Andrew Mort)

**THREE GREAT NEW INTERNATIONAL
CAB-OVER-ENGINE MODELS**
19,500 TO 27,500 LBS. GVW

Although it was unusual in appearance, the Transtar conventional provided improved vision and was instantly recognizable. The Transtar featured a DCO cab with its unusual vent window, with a conventional tilt fibreglass hood.
(Doug Grieve Collection)

The CO-Loadstar was a tilt-forward COE design. More commonly known as the Cargostar, production ended in 1967.
(Doug Grieve Collection)

applying names such as Loadstar, Transtar, Fleetstar and Cargostar.

More new models followed, including the 1969 Transtar conventional, which was immediately recognisable by its unusually-shaped side window designed to improve vision.

The International R190-series had many applications, including seeing duty as an armoured car. Covered in ⅝in steel plate, and weighing more than 70,000lb, it was powered by a 504ci engine. (Andrew Mort)

Kenworth

Kenworth's roots date back to 1912 in Portland, Oregon, and George and Louis Gerlinger Jr who established the Gersix truck company. In 1919 Edgar Worthington bought into the company. Later Harvey Kent also invested in the firm, and in 1923 the company was reincorporated under the name Kenworth.

The company survived the depression and WWII, and, following the deaths of its owners in 1944, Pacific Car and Foundry Company purchased Kenworth. Production was resumed in peacetime, and in 1956 Kenworth introduced its conventional cab 900-series trucks, followed by a full-tilt COE design in 1957. By 1959, Kenworth trucks were also being assembled

Kenworth's 900-series of conventionals carried on into the 1960s, but in 1961 was redesigned. Kenworth was the first manufacturer to replace its traditional butterfly hood with one able to open 90 degrees. Made of fibreglass for light weight, it proved to be a great idea for ease of servicing, and was soon adopted by the industry. Being made of fibreglass it was also easy to make larger in order to fit, bigger, bulkier engines as these were introduced. (Doug Grieve Collection)

Kenworth continued to improve its trucks, and, in 1961, replaced its 500-series with the new, modern COE K-100 model featuring an all-new frame, cab and interior. This is a Canadian-built version that differed only in the addition of 'Canadian' in the nameplate. (Doug Grieve Collection)

in Canada and Mexico. Kenworth used the letter K stemming from Kent for its COE models, and W from Worthington to designate its conventionals.

To remain competitive, in 1961 Kenworth introduced two new models: the W900 conventional, which provided larger cabs and a redesigned instrument panel, and the K100 COE models all featuring a 75-degree tilt, which was designed for maximising cargo within the overall length restrictions imposed by eastern state regulations.

By 1966, Kenworth had forty-six dealers across the US alone, with more outlets around the world. Combined with international sales, Kenworth sold over 3900 trucks during the year – a new high. Sales continued to increase, but did not reach 10,000 units until the early 1970s.

Lectra Haul from 1963

This rather unique American truck builder was established in 1963 by the Unit Rig and Equipment Company of Tulsa, Oklahoma. The company had built oil equipment and some military vehicles in the past before it decided to specialise in a range of dump trucks. In 1963 its 85-ton (75,576kg) dump truck was the largest in the world. Over the decade Lectra Haul constructed larger and larger dump trucks, including a 200-ton (181,440kg) unit. These dump trucks all featured diesel motors with an electric drive via generators powering planetary-geared wheel motors. The suspension was also distinctive, with its dynaflow rubber-cushioned columns.

Mack

The Mack Brothers Company was established in Brooklyn, New York in 1903, but in 1905 the firm relocated to Allentown, Pennsylvania. It built Manhattan trucks, before establishing Mack as a brand name.

By 1954 the Mack Thermodyne diesel engine was standard in the H-series, with a petrol engine being optional. This engine would prove to be a reliable performer and a favourite of Mack customers for years to come.

In 1958 the N-series COE with a tilt-cab was introduced, followed by the G-series ultra-short BBC trucks in 1959. Its upright, short cab design still allowed

Mack introduced its BBC G-series in 1959. Its short cab length took advantage of the greater standardisation in state GCW and overall lengths. It was aimed at West Coast operators. At the same time the all-aluminium cab was also favoured due to its greater driver comfort and ease of maintenance. A 1961 G73 diesel is pictured. (Andrew Mort)

Mack introduced its new off-road M-series trucks in 1961, which replaced the ageing L-series. The M featured tubular front axles, progressive-rate leaf springs, an alloy I-beam steel frame, and oversize radiators. It was a heralded design and selected by the American Society of Industrial Designers for part of the American display at the 1963 International Design Show at the Louvre in Paris. (Doug Grieve Collection)

Mack introduced its new COE F-series in 1962 with an extremely short BBC. It was available with or without a sleeper in lengths of 50, 72 and 80 inches (127, 183, 203cm). Standard engine was the 211hp, END 711 Thermodyne; with or without turbo-charging, but many other engines were optional.
(Andrew Mort)

Many Mack C-series were powered by the new END 864 diesel engine, although other, less powerful engines were available.
(Doug Grieve Collection)

for a wide variety of engines to be fitted to suit the needs of all haulers. First introduced in 1954, the H60 COE series remained in production until 1962.

After displaying versions of the new off-road M-series trucks in 1960, production got underway in 1961. It was a heralded design.

In 1962 Mack unveiled its F-series all-steel COE and conventional trucks in both sleeper and non-sleeper guise. Mack continued to introduce more

trucks, and in 1963 it announced the snub-nosed C, which was based on a standard L-series cab raised and with a shortened B hood and B-series fenders. This cab-forward design – with its engine placed half under the cab and half under the hood – proved to be popular. With its 89in BBC, it could haul a 40-foot trailer and still keep within the legal 50-foot length. Also unveiled at this time was an MB-series of highway and city trucks.

Replacing the N tilting-cab was the clean, straight-cut 1963 MB line; perfect for both highway and city use. There were many engines offered, including a 189hp Chrysler gasoline V8. Pictured is a 1965 model. (Doug Grieve Collection)

In 1965 Mack introduced its new R-series conventional with the idea it would replace the ageing B-series. (Doug Grieve Collection)

In May 1964 Chrysler Corporation announced it was going to buy Mack Trucks Inc as a new division. All the details had been worked-out, but the US government stepped in and threatened them with antitrust violations. As a result, the deal was cancelled.

Two series of trucks were introduced in 1965. The R-series conventionals had big shoes to fill, as they were to gradually replace the B-series. The new U-series featured improved visibility, but also provided a BBC distance similar to the C-series cabs. Both new lines featured a manual tilt-forward moulded hood and fender assembly for easy servicing.

1966 saw the development of the West Coast FL-700-series, which utilised an aluminium F-series cab and other lighter components for use in that market. A similar RL West Coast version followed, and the following year RS and FS models, which featured

The offset cab of the new 1965 Mack U-series was known as the 'Commandcab.' Its distinctive looks were not for cosmetic reasons, but rather for improved visibility, as the cab was slightly raised, moved forward and set over to the left, and featured a larger windscreen. (Doug Grieve Collection)

DM 600 Construction "Work Horse"
12-14 Yd. Dumpers
8-10 Yd. Mixers –
70,000 G.V.W.
Tandem or Tri-Axle

DM 400 Great for 8-10 Yd.
Dumper – 7 Yd. Mixers
25 Yd. Refuse Unit
Gas or Diesel Power

The Mack DM range of 1965 also featured an offset cab and was designed specifically for the construction industry; particularly for dumpers and concrete mixers. (Doug Grieve Collection)

frames fitted with steel side rails. Also unveiled for 1966 was the DM model designed for the construction industry.

Although production continued to increase, so did costs. Profits were minimal, forcing Mack to look for alternative financing and support. In 1967, Mack Trucks, Inc was purchased by the Signal Oil and Gas Company, a Los Angeles based petroleum company.

Mack, which always had a fine reputation for its engines and engineering, announced the new Maxidyne engine in 1967. This new diesel was capable of maximising its horsepower over a wider range of

47,459 examples of the Mack B61 truck were built in its long production, which ended on April 28, 1966. Today, it is still a favourite amongst collectors and truck enthusiasts. (Andrew Mort)

Mack announced its new Maxidyne engine in 1967 and, along with it, the new five-speed Maxitorque transmission. This was the first triple countershaft, compact-length design for Class 8 trucks, and featured one of the highest torque capacities in the industry. The Maxitorque also had a size advantage, as it was only two-thirds the size of the normal multi-speed transmission, so there was also the benefit of significantly less weight. (Andrew Mort)

Only 1619 examples of the Mack B75 were built. The B70 series, with its larger engine compartment, was fitted with the more powerful 672ci Cummins diesel engine favoured by the Midwest and West Coast trucking firms. (Andrew Mort)

engine speeds compared to the competition while providing excellent fuel economy. Due to the flexibility of the engine, a transmission with five forward speeds was more than adequate. This, compared to most diesels that required transmissions with ten or more speeds, was a real advantage in the marketplace. The Maxitorque transmission (TRL 107 series), created in 1967, was the first triple countershaft, compact-length design for class 8 trucks, featuring the highest torque capacity in the industry. The 5-speed Maxitorque was only two-thirds as long as a multi-speed transmission,

and its light weight made it a popular choice among operators concerned about gross vehicle weight.

As the decade ended Mack introduced cab air suspension, which resulted in a vastly improved ride, as well as greater cab durability.

B-753LST

LIGHTWEIGHT • TURBOCHARGED — DIESEL • TRACTOR

Rarer still was the Mack B75 3LS (lightweight model), of which only 456 examples were built. The lightweight models were powered by the Mack Thermodyne engine. (Doug Grieve Collection)

Oshkosh

Oshkosh Motor Truck Manufacturing Company in Oshkosh, Wisconsin was established in 1918. First known for its 4x4 trucks, in the late 1940s Oshkosh introduced its first 6x6 W-series, which continued to evolve throughout the 1950s and was joined by the 50-50-series in 1955, followed by various models utilising International cabs and built until 1966.

By 1960 Oshkosh was building C-, F- and D-series trucks, some with tandem steering front axles and four rear axles for a 12x10 drive.

In 1960 the now familiar Oshkosh look was established, with its forward slanting windscreen, rearward slanting roof, angular fenders, and huge rectangular grille.

The largest Oshkosh models were in its COE 3000 line used mainly for off-road, featuring a one-man offset cab. Introduced in 1962, the U44-L was a conventional 4WD, two-man tandem with offset cab, designed for transporting heavy equipment. The R-series conventional found similar use.

The 50-50 multi-axle versions (known as the 45-45 with diesel power), evolved into the D-series equipped with twin front steering axles, and came in 12x10 drive. The C-, D- and F-series were aimed at the construction industry, and were often built as a rear-discharge concrete carrier.

In 1968 the M-series was introduced, first as a vehicle for military firefighting use, then later for civilian rescue and firefighting applications.

Oshkosh developed many special trucks and super heavy-duty vehicles throughout the 1960s, as well as rebuilding existing vehicles and retro-fitting diesel engines in place of the original gasoline motors for the American military forces.

Peninsula Diesel 1961-62

Peninsula Diesel was a short-lived Canadian truck manufacturer that built approximately ten COE trucks in 1961-62 as a division of parent company Switson Industries Limited of Welland and Toronto, Ontario. Peninsula trucks were powered by a Cummins, Detroit, or Rolls-Royce diesel engine.

Peninsula was a short-lived Canadian truck manufacturer that built a handful of diesel-powered examples in 1961-62 before disappearing from the scene. (Doug Grieve Collection)

Peterbilt continued to improve its trucks throughout the 1960s. The company's reputation for reliability and steady, sound improvements saw production double in the 1960s to 21,000 units over the previous decade. Pictured is a 352 COE. (Doug Grieve Collection)

Peterbilt

Peterbilt was based on what was once Fageol. Despite initial success in the 1950s, a market downturn resulted in lower sales. Pacific Car and Foundry, which already owned Kenworth, purchased Peterbilt Motors on June 24, 1958. One year later, Pacific Car started construction of a modern manufacturing facility in Newark, California. In August 1960, Peterbilt moved to the new facility and became a division of the parent firm.

Peterbilt's tried and true 351 conventional remained both popular and competitive throughout the 1960s. In 1968 the conventional could be ordered with either an aluminium or fibreglass tilting hood. (Doug Grieve Collection)

The Peterbilt 359 evolved directly from the earlier 351 and appeared in 1967. This example was built in 1969. (Andrew Mort)

In 1959 Peterbilt had introduced its new 282 and 352 COE designs, and these proved to be very popular, remaining in production in various forms until 1980. The 282 and 352 models, in particular, received constant updates and upgrades throughout the 1960s. A 1963 facelift, for example, saw the addition of dual headlamps, and a four-piece windscreen featuring curved glass at the corners of the cab. The H versions featured taller cabs and larger radiators.

The model 351 conventional and related versions that were added to the line-up in 1964 continually evolved until 1976. A tilt-hood was introduced in 1965 on the newly designated 288 and 358, but, in 1967, the numerous modifications and redesigns resulted in yet another model number change to 289 and 359.

This 1967 DG830H REO Cummins diesel is believed to be the only example left. (Andrew Mort)

REO to 1967

REO was first established as a car company in 1904 by Ransom E Olds, and in 1910 it introduced its first truck under the name of its subsidiary the REO Motor Truck Company. REO lost money every year from 1930 to 1940 (except for 1933) and these financial difficulties continued following WWII.

Despite more military contracts in the early fifties and attempts to diversify, REO was purchased in 1954 by Bohn Aluminium and Brass Corporation, before being sold to the White Motor Company in 1957. White went on to buy Diamond T in 1958 and production of these trucks was moved to Lancing, Michigan in 1960.

(Both REO and Diamond T were built until 1966 as separate trucks.)

In the 1960s the REO line consisted of the existing C-series, tilt-COE range, which had recently been introduced and was joined by an E-series of medium and heavy-duty conventionals. Yet as the decade progressed, more and more REO heavy-duty trucks were offered in 4x2, 6x4, 6x6 and 8x6 configurations. The largest of these trucks were powered by a 335hp diesel engine.

Following a reorganization in 1967, White announced formation of the new Diamond REO Division.

Built in Montreal, Canada, Sicard trucks were "custom-engineered to individual needs." Sicard advertised that its heavy-duty trucks had GVW ratings from 43,000 to 93,000lb. (Doug Grieve Collection)

Sicard to 1968

Sicard of Ste Therese, Quebec dated back to 1927 and built trucks mainly for snow-clearing and municipal sanitation uses. Sicard also built various series of tractor trailer units throughout its history, but total truck production is estimated at about 2500 units. Very few trucks were built from 1962 onward, and those that were, were chiefly for the PACCAR group (then known as the Pacific Car and Foundry Company), which ultimately took over the firm in 1968.

The Studebaker Transtar tractor trailer unit was similar in appearance to the smaller Transtar models. It was available in various wheelbases, with GVWs in the range of 14.5 tons (13,154kg) to 20.5 tons (18,598kg). (Doug Grieve Collection)

Studebaker to 1964

Although being the major wagon builder that helped to open up the American West in the 19th century, Studebaker was never a major truck manufacturer. It first built electric commercial vehicles before switching to gas in 1913. Still, the company carved out its own niche in the market. During WWII Studebaker built 6x4 and 6x6 Hercules-powered 2.5-ton military trucks.

Throughout the 1950s Studebaker struggled, and for the last three years of the decade annual production was a mere 5000-6000 trucks per year, and that included its popular ½-ton (454kg) pickup models.

In 1961 the Studebaker-Packard Corporation announced it would market a line of medium-duty and heavy-duty trucks and truck tractors powered by diesel engines. When introduced in 1962, these Transtar models could be ordered with the Series 53, 130hp, two-cycle, 4-cylinder diesel engine from General Motors Diesel Division, which had been designed four years earlier. It would be one of the last commercial trucks designed by Studebaker. Studebaker truck production halted in 1964 with the moving of all car production to Hamilton, Ontario.

PROFIT PRODUCING FORMULA FOR TRUCK OPERATORS

NEW STUDEBAKER DIESELS

29,000 TO 42,000 LBS. GCW
10,000 TO 24,000 LBS. GVW

The new Studebaker E35 to E45 was a 96in BBC capable of hauling 40-foot loads in all fifty states. (Doug Grieve Collection)

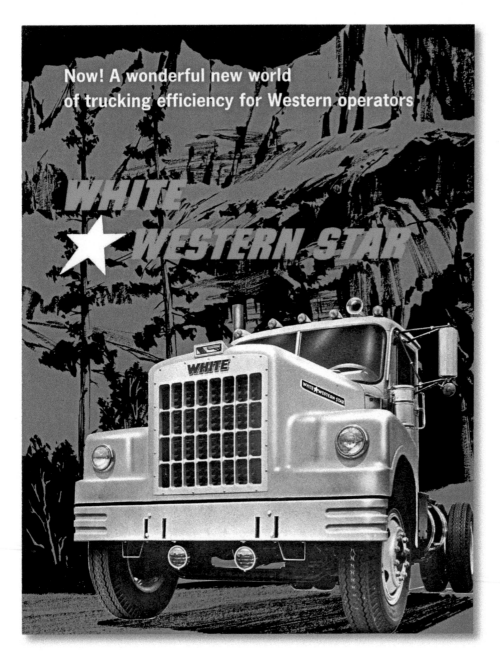

Now! A wonderful new world
of trucking efficiency for Western operators

WHITE

★ WESTERN STAR

Western Star from 1967

Western Star was founded in 1967 in Canada as a subsidiary of White, with the sole purpose of attracting West Coast trucking firms primarily involved in logging where tough, rugged trucks were required. Western Star soon became more widely known – even in Australia – for its reliability, no-nonsense styling, and the use of the best engineering and drivetrains available. The range, which included 6x4 and 6x6 highway trucks, was soon expanded for a broader market. Western Star became independent following Volvo's acquisition of White in 1981.

Western Star proved to be a great success. The company was conceived originally to build trucks for the West Coast. This early brochure touts its great efficiency.
(Doug Grieve Collection)

Western Star was destined to become a 'star' with its line of conventionals, not only on the West Coast, but as far away as Australia also.

White

The White Sewing Machine Company soon abandoned its steam-powered vehicles after being renamed the White Company in 1906. Production of larger, heavy-duty trucks led to its first gas-powered example in 1910. The company flourished, first taking over Sterling and Autocar, and then later in the 1950s REO and Diamond T. At the same time it had a marketing affiliation with Freightliner.

In 1959 the 5000-series was introduced, and production continued into the new decade. White's 5000 COE design utilised fibreglass and aluminium,

White entered the 1960s with its 3000- and 5000-series already established, but continued to expand the line-up of both. This is a White 5000. (Doug Grieve Collection)

MAKING MONEY AT EVERY TURN...

a snapshot story →

White introduced the smaller 1500-series COE with a truck tractor wheelbase of just 74in (188cm). A Perkins 4-cylinder diesel engine version was added, as were half-cab versions. (Doug Grieve Collection)

The new White 7000 line introduced in 1961 featured a lightweight aluminium cab, torsion bar tilt, and a range of engines providing from 180hp to 265hp. (Doug Grieve Collection)

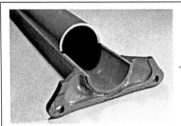

TUBULAR CROSSMEMBER Tube is swedged into attaching flange then welded at outer edge. This provides ultimate stiffness and minimum weight.

VELVET–RIDE Frictionless rubber torsion ring springs isolate chassis from road shock, provide excellent riding qualities under all road conditions.

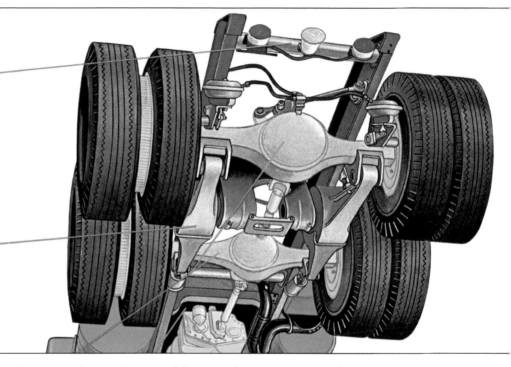

In 1965, White introduced its new 'Velvet-Ride.' Throughout the 1960s White's annual production fluctuated, peaking in 1966 with 32,422 units. Production dropped by nearly 25 per cent the following year, but by 1969 had risen again to 31,520 trucks. While this decade ended on a high note, production would slump again in 1970 by almost a third. Pictured is a White 4000-series, model 4664 TD diesel. (Doug Grieve Collection)

thus saving nearly 2000lb (908kg) in weight. A 1500-series COE compact city truck appeared in 1960. Also in 1960, White began purchasing the half-cab designs and tooling from Cook Bros, added a series of diesel pusher-tandem tractors, and introduced a medium-duty tandem tractor to its line-up. White continued to launch more models and new versions of existing series, particularly the 3000 line. The big news

in 1961 was the 7000-series tilt-cab line, constructed of aluminium with fibreglass trim.

Now known as the White Motor Corporation, in 1965 the company introduced Velvet Ride, featuring a tandem axle suspension using natural rubber springs.

1966 saw a new gasoline engine developed for heavy-duty units, which weighed 40 per cent less than a diesel engine. Also introduced were the 4000 and 9000

The White Mustang V8 engine was loosely based on a Cummins diesel. Rated at 250hp and optional for the 4000- and 9000-series, it proved not to be a popular choice and was discontinued in 1967. Pictured is a 9000TS. (Andrew Mort)

model ranges of heavy-duty trucks featuring fibreglass frame-mounted fenders designed for quick removal and engine servicing. White also bought the Hercules Engine Division from the Hupp Corporation in 1966.

By 1967 there was little to distinguish White's Diamond T and REO trucks. Consequently, the two old nameplates and subsidiaries were finally merged. White continued to expand, and acquired the Alco engine line from Studebaker-Worthington in 1969.

Americans at work

Throughout the 1960s the trucking industry was called upon to build bigger and bigger trucks. The main sources of these demands were the American military for the war in Vietnam, the construction industry for its building of skyscrapers, towers and city apartments, and NASA for hauling rockets etc in the space race.

The industry responded, and soon weights that were unimagined even in the 1950s were being carried by trucks to fulfill all manner of needs.

Specialised trucks were very profitable when the design proved sound. For example, in 1964 Freightliner introduced the half-cab for off-road construction. (Courtesy Freightliner)

Despite the industry's rather slow acceptance of diesel engines, approximately 75 per cent of the Mack trucks delivered after 1959 were fitted with a diesel engine. After 1960 Mack concentrated on only developing diesel engines for its trucks. (Andrew Mort)

No: 40335
Model: CK64 Half-Cab
        Photograph is generally representative of this model chassis,
        but does not necessarily represent a chassis of standard
        specifications.

Autocar entered the half-cab market later than most in the 1960s. Half-cabs were generally used for construction, and became more and more popular throughout the decade. (Doug Grieve Collection)

These Autocar DC9964s were powered by 220hp diesel engines with a 16,000lb capacity front axle. Here, an Eastern Shore Transit Mix is hard at work in Waretown, New Jersey. (Doug Grieve Collection)

Niche markets continued to be developed by some manufacturers to cater to specialised areas – most commonly the construction industry, or for off-road use.

However, it was the overall prosperity of the decade, and the subsequent demand by consumers for more

and more goods, that the trucking industry had difficulty keeping pace with.

While the number of truck manufacturers shrank – mostly due to competition – the trucking market in America continued to grow throughout the 1960s.

In 1964 Mack production was 12,064 units. Out of that total, 10,353 of those Mack trucks had a GVW of over 33,000lb (14,969kg), and another 1432 had a GVW between 26,000lb (11,794kg) and 33,000lb (14,969kg). (Andrew Mort)

The heavy-duty truck market had begun the decade in a bit of a slump, but in 1962 sales increased by 35 per cent as diesel engines and new designs began to generate sales. At the same time old favourites, such as Ford's C-series and Mack's B61, shown here, continued to sell well. (Andrew Mort)

Despite the increasing demand for diesels – up 29 per cent in 1963 – overall, gas engines still ruled the truck industry. Pictured is a 1963 Autocar-Diesel DC-87. (Andrew Mort)

In the 1960s truck interiors became more comfortable and better equipped, as can be seen from this photograph of the International Fleetstar 2000 interior. (Andrew Mort)

BIG-TRUCK DURABILITY . . .
DEEP-DOWN COMFORT

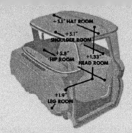

SPACIOUS CABS provide extra inches of space. At shoulder level there's 5" more room, and there's nearly 6" more hiproom. In spite of lower outside measurements, you get more headroom and legroom too.

EXTRA SAFETY VISION is offered by the new windshield that is 26% larger. Electric windshield wipers cover 38% more area for greater safety.

STURDY DEEP-COMFORT TRUCK SEAT† offers 5½" more width and is exceptionally durable. Combination of S-wire, coil and flat spring construction is topped by a thick foam pad, for a more comfortable, controlled ride.

† With auxiliary transmission, driver's and auxiliary seats are supplied in place of full width seat.

Every new G.M.C. Comfort-King cab is engineered for tough "on-the-road" service . . . and long-lasting newness. Double-wall, High-Level ventilation cowl housings form an arch structure of very rugged design at the front of the cab. Box-section door pillars strengthen the side panels. And new "Z"-bar sills tie the cab together securely, fore and aft. Improved door fit, hinging, sealing and latching, as well as the thick insulation between the cab's double roof panels, and resilient 4-point rubber cab mounting, are all typical of "built-to-last" comfort for added driver efficiency.

As early as 1960, GMC began stressing greater comfort, safety and durability in its trucks. Trucking for the driver was

American ingenuity in the 1960s

Although considered a more modern 'green' idea, the search for alternative power began well before the 1990s in the transportation industry. The concept of turbine engine power dates back to the 1950s, as do alternative fuels.

Chevrolet demonstrated this when it showcased its Turbo Titan III, which featured not only a gas-turbine engine, but also an automatic transmission, a power tilt-cab, and such comforts as power windows, a CB set and stereo, plus stylish hideaway headlamps. It had evolved from the Turbo Titan II, which was first unveiled in 1965.

the new
MACK 255 hp
V-8 Thermodyne Diesel

After almost six years of development work Mack introduced its END 864 V8 diesel engine in 1962. Rated at 255hp, Mack was secure in the fact that this lightweight V8 could haul any load at maximum speed anywhere in America.
(Doug Grieve Collection)

Throughout the 1960s new materials, better assembly, and easier servicing led to fresh design concepts.
(Doug Grieve Collection)

Fuller® 15-Speed RT-12515 Series Roadranger® Transmissions

*For operating on all types of terrain with engines up to 450 hp. and loads up to 130,000 lbs. G.C.W.**

The Fuller Roadranger transmission featured a twin counter-shaft providing both a low side and high side in one box. Even today this Fuller transmission is one of the only manual gearbox transmissions offered. (Doug Grieve Collection)

Despite a wide variety of engineering attempts, it would not be a new truck engine that would revolutionise trucking in the 1960s, but rather the concepts of containerisation and piggybacking – specifically, the increasing use of containerisation coupled with the interchangeability of trailer designs to allow for the

Over the decade more and more manufacturers opted for tandem axle drive over the traditional single drive for handling the heavier loads, giving greater traction and eventually better resale value. (Andrew Mort)

transport of goods by highway, rail and air-opened markets, not only all over North America, but all over the world, with minimal handling.

Some interesting ideas proved to be failures in the marketplace, such as Apex Fibreglass Products' transparent fibreglass fuel tank, which allowed drivers to check the level without the use of a gauge. Overall though, the American trucking industry never lacked ingenuity, and it experimented with new ideas and technology throughout the decade. The images here are only a sample of this.

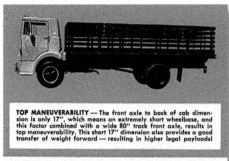

TOP MANEUVERABILITY — The front axle to back of cab dimension is only 17", which means an extremely short wheelbase, and this factor combined with a wide 80" track front axle, results in top maneuverability. This short 17" dimension also provides a good transfer of weight forward — resulting in higher legal payloads!

FRAME, AXLES, TRANSMISSIONS — As on all of our new Diamond T models, our Trend frame rails are full depth, without taper, from front to rear. This rail measures 9¼" x 3" x ¼". Note the common heavy channel crossmembers used throughout. Transmissions and axles used have been on the market for a number of years and are proven components.

LONG LIFE — HIGH RESALE VALUE — The Diamond T Trend cab is of Royalex. Doors are steel, heavily treated with zinc. The cab offers full three man seating, a "walk-through" floor, is easy to repair, and has excellent insulating qualities. These features offer high resale value.

While some innovations proved to be industry trend-setting, others, such as GMC and Chevrolet's independent air front and rear air stabiliser didn't. Although considered a breakthrough in 1960, by 1963 this air suspension system was dropped. Pictured is a GMC DLR8000 featuring this short-lived innovation. (Doug Grieve Collection)

The introduction of 'doubles,' or hauling two trailers behind one tractor, has often been referred to as one of the most important innovations in trucking history. (Doug Grieve Collection)

Diamond REO introduced four new models in its 'Trend' line in 1968. (The name had been used in the past by White and its other divisions.) One of the big features of this COE model was its Royalex plastic cab first seen in 1966, which resisted corrosion and dents. Diamond T press releases noted that heat alone "popped out" most dents, and there was a lower cost in plastic repair for more extensive damage. (Doug Grieve Collection)

In 1960 gasoline 6-cylinder engines were fitted in 70 per cent of the trucks built, while 24 per cent were gasoline V8s. The remaining per cent were gasoline 4-cylinder engines, or diesel units. The growth in demand for diesel engines during this decade changed the industry dramatically, as more and more truck manufacturers would seek a diesel proprietary engine. In 1960, Cummins dominated the diesel engine market with a 60 per cent holding. (Andrew Mort)

Specialisation continued to be stressed in the 1960s, especially by the smaller manufacturers who found profits in niche markets. Hendrickson had survived for decades catering to specialised markets, as this November 1961 advertisement stresses. (Doug Grieve Collection)

LEADERSHIP Thru the Century

Mr. M. Hendrickson began designing and building motor trucks and automobiles at the turn of the century. The friction-drive truck at right was built in 1907.

For many years the Hendrickson organization has been headed by the four Hendrickson brothers. Now aided by the third generation, Hendrickson has maintained leadership in the automotive industry by strict adherence to the highest standards of reliability and performance.

MOTOR TRUCK DIVISION

This COE tilt-cab truck was built by M. Hendrickson in 1912, for a Boston dealer.

Quite different in appearance, size, and performance from its 1912 predecessor, this 1961 Hendrickson COE Tractor incorporates the newest adaptations of tested designs.

SPECIAL EQUIPMENT DIVISION

This 1927 Hendrickson custom-built Crane Carrier was designed for a 7½-ton crane.

Current Crane Carriers are manufactured for cranes from 10-ton to over 60-ton capacities.

TANDEM DIVISION

This first practical tandem axle suspension, designed and built by Hendrickson in 1926, featured parallelogram design and the exclusive below-axle walking beam.

Modern Hendrickson Tandem Suspensions are available with Steel Spring, Rubber Load Cushion, and Air Ride springing media. Equalizing beams distribute loads evenly to both axles and reduce the effects of road irregularities 50%; torque rods and rubber bushings absorb starting and braking torque and eliminate maintenance; vertical drive pins leave the springs free to perform the sole function of cushioning the load.

HENDRICKSON Manufacturing Company, Lyons, Illinois

88   *For more information circle 88 on Reader Service Card*   *For more information circle 89 on Reader Service Card*➝

FWD introduced its ForWarD Mover COE in 1968, and its many novel mechanical features found favour in the construction

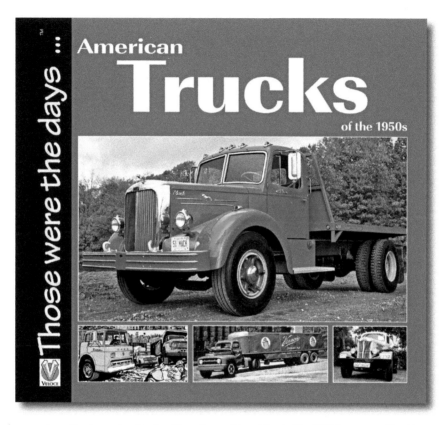

This highly visual study examines the important role of trucks and trucking in the 1950s, recounting the essential role it played in the industrial growth of the US and Canada. Features factory photos, advertisements, original truck brochures and restored examples, plus a comprehensive guide to all models produced.

ISBN: 978-1-84584-227-7

For more info on Veloce titles, visit our website at www.veloce.co.uk
email info@veloce.co.uk • tel: +44 (0)1305 260068

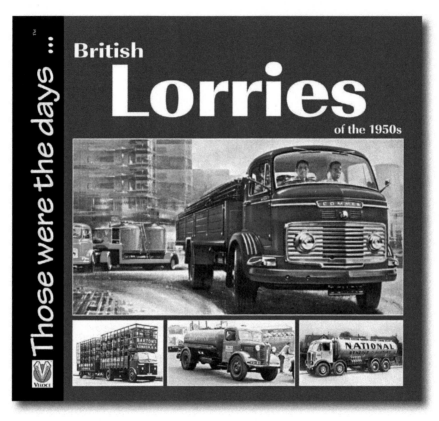

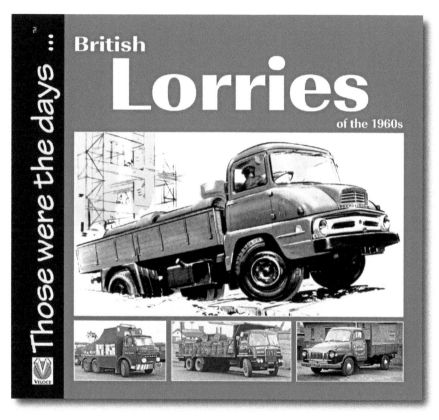

A highly visual look at British lorries produced during the 1960s. Familiar and less familiar names connected with the road haulage industry are covered, with comprehensive text revealing much about these productive and essential vehicles.

ISBN: 978-1-84584-211-6

For more info on Veloce titles, visit our website at www.veloce.co.uk
email info@veloce.co.uk • tel: +44 (0)1305 260068

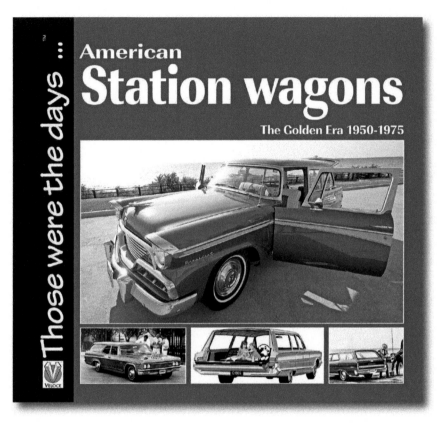

This book examines the important quarter century period when the American station wagon was a family standard and status symbol of a successful suburban lifestyle, recounting its essential role in North American society in the '50s, '60s and '70s.

ISBN: 978-1-845842-68-0

For more info on Veloce titles, visit our website at www.veloce.co.uk
email info@veloce.co.uk • tel: +44 (0)1305 260068

Index